D0117053

simply
Atlantic
Seafood

© 2006 Silverback Books, Inc.

All rights reserved. No part of this book
may be reproduced in any form without
the written permission of the publisher.

Project Editor: Lisa M. Tooker
Editor: Lynda Zuber Sassi
Layout & Production: Patty Holden
Photography & Recipes: StockFood

Printed in China

ISBN: 1-59637-051-3

Table of Contents

The World of Seafood

For centuries, people of all cultures have found the sustenance provided by fish and shellfish to be a vital part of their diet. The Romans used to trade for fertilized fish eggs that were then used for farming fish. For centuries, the Chinese have efficiently used their flooded rice fields for fish farming. The French began harvesting mussels for culinary purposes in the 13th century, and as far back as 1520, fish tacos were recorded as a staple of the Mexican diet. Today, between health benefits, countless varieties and ways to prepare, and quick cooking times, fish and shellfish have become the quintessential modern meal.

Basics

Health

At one time, preparing seafood for family and friends was a daunting proposition to the home chef. However, during the past decade, seafood has worked its way to become a mainstay in the American diet. And it's no wonder, the health benefits of eating fish rank higher than just about any other type of protein. The Omega-3 fatty acids found in fish have proven to be helpful in lowering the risk of coronary artery disease as well as a host of other health issues and diseases. The FDA recommends that we consume at least three servings of fish each week, a task that has become manageable given the increased availability and freshness of fish in most local grocery stores.

Sustainability

In a book about seafood, it would be remiss not to touch upon the concerns of rising mercury levels and sustainability of seafood populations. As a consumer, you have the ability to make informed decisions about what you eat. Bring a chart of the mercury levels in fish with you to the grocery store and select fish with low mercury levels like scallops, sole, or wild salmon. Ask where the fish you are buying came from and consider spending a little more on fish that was line caught, or wild, by fishermen who practice sustainable habits. Individually, we can impact the whole and make a difference through our purchasing power.

Ingredients

The recipes in this book explore a variety of fish and shellfish types. Ranging from popular and well known fish like halibut and salmon, to more exotic bivalves like oysters, that most people would shy away from making at home. Each chapter focuses on a particular type of fish or shellfish and provides both classic and contemporary recipes, ranging from a traditional New England Clam Chowder, Grilled Shrimp, and Oysters on the Half Shell, to recipes with pizzazz, like Blackened Salmon with Avocado and Mango Salsa, Thai Noodle Salad with Scallops, and Risotto with Lobster.

Now it is up to you, the guidance and inspiration is found in the recipes on the following pages. So select one or two, visit your fishmonger, make an informed decision, and savor the benefits that come from making seafood a staple in your diet.

Fish

The myth that preparing fish is difficult is simply false. With hundreds of varieties, and many of them interchangeable, finding a good piece of fish is no longer a challenge. Before buying, carefully examine the fish. Check for fillets or steaks that are moist, shiny, and firm and whole fish that have glistening scales, clear eyes, and pink gills. Avoid fish that smells bad, or has a dull, lackluster appearance. It is always a good idea to get to know your fishmonger and ask him to make recommendations. And, if ever a choice to buy wild or line caught fish, indulge, the flavor will be unrivaled.

For best results and to ensure freshness, buy fish within 24 hours of when you plan to serve it. Preparing fish can be as simple as rinsing and drying it, and seasoning with salt, pepper, and a little olive oil, or introducing other flavor combinations such as those found in the recipes in this chapter. Fish can be cooked using a number of techniques, from steaming, to grilling, to baking. Fish cooks quickly, so be sure to keep an eye on the time to avoid overcooking. Even the freshest fish won't be a palette pleaser if it is rubbery and dry.

Fried Sole with Caper Sauce

Serves 4:

Caper sauce:
1 small shallot
1 clove garlic
2 tablespoons butter
2 teaspoons lemon juice
½ cup white wine
½ cup heavy cream
2 tablespoons capers, drained

Fried sole:
4 sole fillets (6–8 ounces each)
1 cup all-purpose flour
1 teaspoon baking powder
½ cup cornstarch
1 cup water
2 teaspoons sea salt
1 teaspoon olive oil
Vegetable oil
Freshly ground black pepper

FOR CAPER SAUCE: Peel shallots and garlic and dice finely. In a heavy saucepan, melt butter over medium heat. Add garlic and shallots and sauté until lightly browned, then add lemon juice and wine. Boil until liquid is reduced to half. Add cream and stir constantly with a wooden spoon until reduced to half. Add capers, lower the heat, and simmer for 5 more minutes. Remove sauce from heat and set aside until ready to serve over sole.

FOR FRIED SOLE: Rinse sole, pat dry, and season with salt and pepper.

In a bowl, combine flour, baking powder, cornstarch, water, salt, olive oil, and pepper until there are no lumps.

Heat vegetable oil in a deep fryer or deep pot over medium heat to 375°F.

Dredge sole through the batter, then place in the hot oil one piece at a time. Try to keep the pieces from touching one another until the batter has set. Cook until batter turns golden brown. Then remove sole and drain on a paper towel.

Place a piece of sole on each plate and drizzle caper sauce over the top. Serve julienned carrots and rice pilaf on the side.

Mediterranean Stuffed Sole

Serves 4:

4 sole fillets (6–8 ounces each)
1 small onion
3 cloves garlic
2 medium tomatoes
2 sprigs fresh marjoram
2 tablespoons extra virgin olive oil
½ cup pitted, chopped kalamata olives
½ cup breadcrumbs
⅓ cup freshly grated Parmigiano-Reggiano cheese
Salt (preferably kosher or sea)
Freshly ground black pepper

Preheat oven to 350°F.

Rinse sole, pat dry, and season with salt and pepper.

Peel and chop onion and garlic. Rinse tomatoes, remove the seeds, and dice. Rinse marjoram, dry, remove the leaves, and chop finely. Heat 1 tablespoon of olive oil in a medium skillet until very hot, then add the onion and garlic and sauté for 1–2 minutes. Add tomatoes and marjoram, toss with onions, and sauté for 2 more minutes. Remove from heat, let cool.

Place cooled tomato mixture in bowl and add olives, breadcrumbs, and Parmigiano-Reggiano, mixing well. Spoon stuffing into the center of each piece of sole and wrap ends around it. Place seam side down in a baking dish and bake in the oven for 15–20 minutes until sole flakes easily.

Serve sole on top of tomatoes and garnish with extra chopped marjoram.

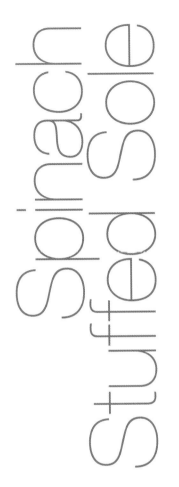

Spinach Stuffed Sole

Serves 4:

4 sole fillets (6–8 ounces each)
1 small onion
1 clove garlic
1 cup fresh spinach
2 basil leaves
1 teaspoon extra virgin olive oil
2 tablespoons sherry
Salt (preferably kosher or sea)
Freshly ground black pepper

Preheat oven to 400 ºF.

Rinse sole, pat dry, and season with salt and pepper.

Coat a 10 x 6 inch baking dish with nonstick cooking spray.

Peel onion and garlic and chop finely. Rinse spinach and basil and chop. Heat oil in a skillet and sauté onions and garlic for 3 minutes or until tender. Add spinach and continue cooking for about 1 minute or until spinach is barely wilted. Remove from heat and drain liquid into prepared baking dish.

Add basil to vegetables and stir together. Divide vegetables evenly and place in center of each piece of sole. Roll each fillet around the spinach, place seam-side down in baking dish, and season with sherry, salt, and pepper. Bake for 15–20 minutes or until sole flakes easily. Lift out with slotted spoon.

Serve with mashed potatoes and tomato sauce on the side.

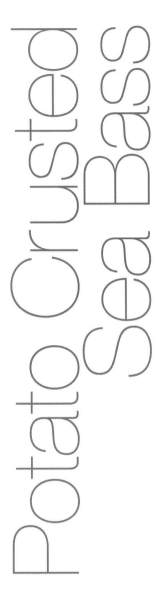
Potato Crusted Sea Bass

Serves 4:

Tomato tartar sauce:
2 Italian plum tomatoes
1 dill pickle
1 green onion
1 large egg
1¾ cups extra virgin olive oil
Pinch of red pepper flakes
1 teaspoon salt
Sea bass:
2 red potatoes
8 cloves garlic
2 eggs, beaten
4 tablespoons flour
1 teaspoon extra virgin olive oil
4 sea bass fillets (6–8 ounces each)
Salt (preferably kosher or sea)
Freshly ground black pepper

TOMATO TARTER SAUCE: Rinse tomato, remove seeds, and dice. Finely chop pickle. Rinse onion and slice into fine rings. Combine the egg and oil in a blender or food processor and process until it has the consistency of a light mayonnaise, about 3 minutes. Pour into a bowl and fold in tomatoes, pickle, onion, red pepper flakes, and salt, stirring until thoroughly blended. Store in the refrigerator until ready to use, up to two days.

Preheat oven to 375°F.

SEA BASS: Peel potatoes and grate into shoestrings. Peel garlic and mince. Combine potatoes, garlic, eggs, and flour, and season with salt and pepper.

Rub sea bass with potatoes, thoroughly coating the top and sides. Place on a platter, cover loosely, and refrigerate for 30 minutes.

Heat olive oil in an ovenproof sauté pan. Place sea bass, potato side down, in the pan and cook for 5 minutes. Turn the fish over and cook for 3 minutes. Place pan into the oven and cook for 10–15 minutes.

Remove sea bass from the oven, arrange on warm plates, and drizzle tomato tarter sauce over the top.

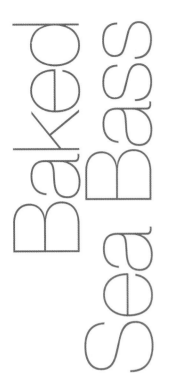

Baked Sea Bass

Serves 4:

4 sea bass fillets (6–8 ounces each)
½ cup lemon juice
½ bunch fresh Italian parsley
2 cloves garlic
½ cup butter
½ cup dry white wine

Preheat oven to 350°F.

Rinse sea bass and pat dry. Rinse parsley, dry, remove leaves, and chop finely. Peel garlic and mince. In a bowl, combine parsley, garlic, and lemon juice. Thoroughly coat sea bass on all sides with the marinade. Cover and refrigerate for 30 minutes, turning once.

Melt butter in 13 x 9 x 2 inch baking pan. Place sea bass in the pan. Whisk wine into the marinade and pour over the sea bass. Bake in the oven for 10 minutes, basting once with pan juices.

Remove sea bass from the oven, arrange on warm plates, and drizzle juices over the top. Serve with steamed summer squash, radishes, and green beans.

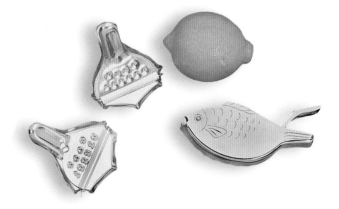

Sea Bass
Wrapped in Bacon

Serves 2:

2 sea bass fillets (6–8 ounces each)
4 bacon slices
1 tablespoon extra virgin olive oil
¼ cup dry white wine
Sea salt
Freshly ground black pepper

Rinse sea bass, pat dry, and season with salt and pepper. Roll or fold each piece of fish so that it looks like a small roast, and wrap 2 slices of bacon around it, securing the pieces of bacon with a toothpick, or cooking twine so the fish is almost completely covered with the bacon (except at the ends).

In a heavy-bottomed skillet, heat olive oil over medium heat. When the pan is hot, add sea bass and brown on all sides, about 6 minutes. Add the wine, cover, and continue cooking until it is cooked through, about 15 minutes, turning once.

Once done, transfer the sea bass to a warm serving platter and let it sit for about 4 minutes. Remove the toothpicks or cooking twine and drain any juices.

To serve, cut the sea bass in half with a very sharp knife. Place atop stewed white beans and steamed spinach.

Baked Cod
with Potatoes

Serves 2:

½ pound Yukon gold potatoes
2 cod fillets (6–8 ounces each)
4 sprigs fresh dill
2 tablespoons lemon juice
Juice of 1 orange
Salt (preferably kosher or sea)
Freshly ground black pepper
2 orange slices
Dill tips

Preheat oven to 325°F.

Boil potatoes in salted water for about 25 minutes.

Rinse cod, pat dry, and lay each one on a piece of aluminum foil that is twice its size. Rinse dill, dry, and chop finely. Sprinkle each piece of cod with dill, drizzle with orange and lemon juice, and season with salt and pepper. Fold the aluminum foil over the cod and seal. Cook in the oven for about 15 minutes.

In the meantime, drain the potatoes, refresh in cold water, then peel, and season with salt and pepper.

Serve cod with its sauce drizzled over the top, and potatoes on warm plates and garnish with orange slices and dill tips.

Olive and Tomato Crusted Cod

Serves 4:

4 thick cod fillets (6–8 ounces each)
1 small onion
2 medium-sized tomatoes
4 sprigs fresh Italian parsley
½ cup chopped black olives
About ½ cup olive oil
1 pound small tomatoes (about 5 or 6)
1 pound green beans
Salt (preferably sea or kosher)
Freshly ground black pepper

Preheat oven to 425°F.

Rinse cod, pat dry, and season with salt and pepper. Peel and chop onion. Rinse tomatoes, remove seeds, and dice. Rinse parsley, dry, remove leaves, and chop finely. In a bowl, combine onion, tomatoes, parsley and olives, and season with salt and pepper. Press onto the cod until coated thoroughly. Drizzle with a little olive oil and lay on a baking sheet lined with aluminum foil.

Wash the small tomatoes, dry, and brush with a little olive oil. Place on the baking sheet with the cod and bake in the oven for 12–15 minutes.

In the meantime, wash and trim the green beans and cook in boiling, salted water for about 10 minutes so they're crunchy, but cooked through.

Serve cod with baked tomatoes and green beans on the side.

Cod with Lemon-Parmesan Crust

Serves 4:

4 cod fillets (6–8 ounces each)
2 teaspoons freshly squeezed lemon juice
1 tablespoon olive oil
1 small onion
2 tablespoons butter
½ cup Italian breadcrumbs
½ pound green beans
2 tablespoons freshly grated Parmigiano-Reggiano
Salt (preferably kosher or sea)
Freshly ground black pepper

Preheat oven to 400°F.

Rinse cod, pat dry, and season with salt and pepper. Combine lemon juice and olive oil in a bowl. Add the cod and coat both sides with the marinade; let stand for 5–10 minutes.

Peel onion and chop. Heat 1 tablespoon of butter in a small frying pan, sauté onions until well done, then combine with breadcrumbs, and remaining butter.

Coat a baking sheet with cooking spray or oil. Using tongs, place the cod on the baking sheet with skin (or darkest) side down. Sprinkle top of each fillet with the breadcrumb mixture. Bake on the center oven shelf for 15 minutes.

In the meantime, steam green beans until crisp, about 5 minutes.

To serve, arrange beans on each plate. Place a piece of cod on top of the beans and sprinkle with Parmigiano-Reggiano.

Halibut with Mango Salsa

Serves 4:

4 halibut steaks (6–8 ounces each)

Halibut marinade:
1 piece ginger
2 cloves garlic
½ of 1 jalapeño pepper
1 cup orange juice
2 limes, juiced
2 tablespoon soy sauce
2 teaspoons extra virgin olive oil

Mango salsa:
6–8 sprigs fresh cilantro
1 firm, ripe mango
½ teaspoon grated ginger
1 tablespoon lime juice
Sea salt

Coconut citrus sauce:
1 clove garlic
½ of 1 jalapeño pepper
½ cup orange juice
2 teaspoons lime juice
1 tablespoon honey
2 slices ginger
½ cup coconut milk
Sea salt

Preheat gas grill to medium-high or charcoal grill to medium-hot coals.

HALIBUT MARINADE: Rinse halibut, pat dry, and season with salt and pepper. Peel ginger and slice crosswise into 4–5 pieces. Peel garlic and mince. Slice jalapeño in half, remove seeds, and mince. Combine marinade ingredients in a 9 x 13 inch glass baking pan. Add halibut, cover, and refrigerate for 20 minutes, turning once.

MANGO SALSA: While halibut is marinating, rinse cilantro, dry, remove leaves, and chop finely. Cut mango into ½ inch cubes. Combine all salsa ingredients in a bowl. Cover and refrigerate.

COCONUT CITRUS SAUCE: Peel and lightly crush garlic. Remove seeds from jalapeño and mince finely. Combine garlic, jalapeño, orange juice, lime juice, honey, and ginger in a saucepan over medium heat. Bring to a boil and reduce heat to low. Simmer for 5 minutes, then remove from heat. Remove garlic and ginger pieces, stir in coconut milk, and season to taste with salt. Cover and keep warm.

Remove halibut from the marinade and place on an oiled grill. Cook until lightly browned on both sides and just opaque, 3–5 minutes per side. To serve, place a piece of halibut in each bowl, pour the sauce around it, and top with mango salsa.

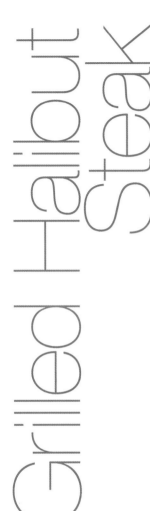

Grilled Halibut Steak

Serves 4:

4 halibut steaks (6–8 ounces each)
6–8 sprigs fresh Italian parsley
1 clove garlic
2 tablespoons freshly squeezed lemon juice
½ teaspoon extra virgin olive oil
Salt (preferably kosher or sea)
Freshly ground black pepper

Rinse halibut, pat dry, and season with salt and pepper.

Rinse parsley, dry, remove leaves, and chop finely. Peel garlic and mince. In a small bowl, combine parsley, garlic, lemon juice, and olive oil. Rub into the halibut and marinate for 10 minutes.

Heat an outdoor grill or grill pan. Grill halibut for 8–12 minutes or until it flakes easily with a fork, turning once.

Serve sprinkled with chopped parsley and lemon wedges.

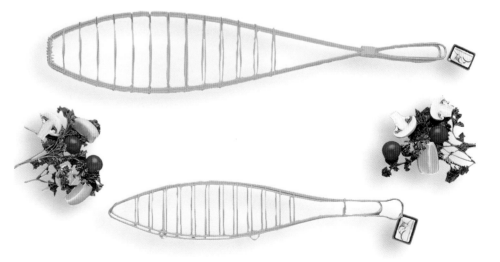

Sweet and Sour Halibut

Serves 4:

4 halibut steaks (6–8 ounces each)
2 tablespoons extra virgin olive oil
1 small red bell pepper
1 small green bell pepper
2 scallions
2 cloves garlic
½ cup water
½ cup brown sugar
3 tablespoons cider vinegar
1 tablespoon soy sauce
½ teaspoon freshly grated ginger
Salt (preferably kosher or sea)
Freshly ground black pepper

Rinse halibut, pat dry, and season with salt and pepper.

Coat grill grate or a grill pan with 1 teaspoon olive oil and preheat.

Rinse peppers, cut in half, remove seeds, and slice thinly. Rinse scallions and cut into 2 inch strips. Peel garlic and mince.

In a medium-sized skillet, heat remaining olive oil, add peppers, and sauté until slightly tender, about 3 minutes.

In a large, non-reactive bowl, combine water, brown sugar, vinegar, soy sauce, garlic, and ginger, then add to the skillet and simmer.

Grill halibut until desired doneness, about 5 minutes per side.

Arrange halibut on warm plates and spoon sweet and sour sauce over top. Serve with a side of rice.

Salmon and Basil Canapés

Makes 16 pieces:

8 ounces smoked salmon, sliced
1 avocado
½ cup onion
4 ounces cream cheese
½ cup sour cream
½ cup mayonnaise
16 pumpernickel rounds, thinly sliced
16 basil leaves

Slice salmon into 16 pieces. Remove avocado pit and spoon the flesh into a food processor bowl. Peel and finely dice onion and add to the bowl along with cream cheese, sour cream, and mayonnaise. Process all ingredients until smooth.

Spread avocado mixture on pumpernickel slices and top with a slice of salmon and a basil leaf.

Cucumber Soup
with Salmon and Dill

Serves 2:

1 cucumber
½ cup plain yogurt
2 tablespoons heavy cream
2 tablespoons sour cream
2 teaspoons lemon juice
½ pound salmon fillet
½ teaspoon ground coriander
1 tablespoon butter
4 sprigs fresh dill
Salt (preferably kosher or sea)
Freshly ground black pepper

Wash and peel cucumber and cut in half lengthwise. Remove seeds with a spoon and cut into rough pieces. Salt lightly and leave for 10 minutes. Pour off cucumber juice and blend cucumber to a purée, adding yogurt, cream, sour cream, and lemon juice. Season with salt and pepper. Cover and refrigerate.

Rinse salmon and dry. Cut into ½ inch cubes. Season with salt, pepper, and coriander. Melt butter in a frying pan and fry the salmon on all sides for 4–5 minutes.

Rinse dill, dry, and chop finely. Remove cucumber soup from the refrigerator and stir in dill. Ladle into 2 bowls, add the salmon, and garnish with additional dill.

Blackened Salmon
with Avocado and Mango Salsa

Serves 4:

Mango salsa:
1 avocado
1 mango
4 sprigs fresh cilantro
½ cup freshly squeezed lime juice
Salt (preferably kosher or sea)
Blackened salmon:
4 salmon fillets (6-8 ounces each)
½ cup ancho chili powder
½ cup kosher salt
2 tablespoons freshly ground black pepper
Extra virgin olive oil
Frisée or mixed greens

MANGO SALSA: Remove pit from avocado and slice into ½ inch cubes. Peel mango and slice into ½ inch cubes. Rinse cilantro, dry, remove leaves, and chop finely. In a bowl, combine avocado, mango, cilantro, and lime juice and season with salt. Toss gently and garnish with cilantro sprigs. Cover and refrigerate.

BLACKENED SALMON: Preheat outdoor grill to medium heat and oil the grates using a brush or paper towel.

Combine chili powder, salt, and pepper in a small bowl. Coat each piece of salmon with a light layer of olive oil and pat the chili mixture on all sides. Place each piece flesh side down on the hot grill and cook for 3–5 minutes per side.

Arrange frisée or mixed greens on each plate, set a piece of salmon in the middle, and a spoonful of salsa on top.

Fettuccini with Salmon and Asparagus

Serves 4:

1 pound fresh fettuccini pasta
½ pound thin green asparagus
4 skinless salmon fillets (6-8 ounces each)
2 tablespoons extra virgin olive oil
1½ cups heavy cream
3 teaspoons grated lemon rind (organic, if possible)
4 ounces smoked salmon, thinly sliced
Salt (preferably kosher or sea)
Freshly ground black pepper

Cook fettuccini in 4–5 quarts of boiling, salted water until al dente. Drain and set aside 1 cup of the cooking water.

Rinse asparagus, cut off the ends, and cook in boiling, salted water for about 8 minutes. Drain and set aside.

Rinse salmon, pat dry, and season with salt and pepper. Heat olive oil in a frying pan and fry the salmon for about 2 minutes on each side.

In a medium pan, bring the cream to a rolling boil, add the lemon rind, and season with salt and pepper. Stir in asparagus, adding some of the cooking water if necessary, then stir in the fettuccini, and season again.

Arrange the fettuccni and asparagus on 4 plates. Place a piece of salmon on top of the fettuccini and garnish with smoked salmon.

Sesame Crusted Salmon

Serves 4:

4 salmon fillets (6–8 ounces each)
½ cup extra virgin olive oil
Salt (preferably kosher or sea)
Freshly ground black pepper
½ cup mixed black and white sesame seeds

Rinse salmon, pat dry, rub with 2 teaspoons olive oil, and season with salt and pepper. Spread sesame seeds in a pie plate and press salmon into the seeds to coat evenly on all sides.

Heat the remaining oil in a heavy bottomed skillet over medium-high heat. Carefully add salmon. Cook 3–5 minutes per side or until desired doneness. Carefully remove salmon from pan, so as not to break the sesame crust.

Serve salmon garnished with lemon wedges. This recipe can also be baked in the oven.

Shrimp and Lobster

Shrimp can be found in multiple variations. It comes in different sizes; it can be found fresh or frozen, shell on or off, cooked or uncooked, making it the most versatile seafood darling of Americans. Unless you can find fresh shrimp, which is rare, buy frozen shrimp over thawed shrimp. Frozen shrimp can last for up to a month, while thawed shrimp will only last for a couple of days. Shrimp and Avocado Bruschetta (p. 48) is the perfect, elegant appetizer, a Shrimp Salad (p. 52) packs a punch, and Grilled Shrimp (p. 50) on the barbeque melts in the mouth with rich, buttery, hot off the grill flavors. No wonder we have a love affair with this crustacean.

Lobster is the more expensive cousin of the shrimp. Also versatile, Lobster with Parmesan Risotto (p. 66) can be served to impress at an elegant meal, as easily as lobster can take on a casual role at a New England Clam Bake (p. 88). Buy lobster fresh, out of the tank, where it should flip its tail and kick its legs upon emerging from the water, or have it flown to your doorstep from the fisherman, a practice that is becoming more popular and ensures freshness. Since you are likely paying top dollar, you want to ensure the highest quality. Plan on a minimum of 1½ pounds of lobster per person and keep in mind that a 3 pound lobster usually has more meat than 2–1½ pound lobsters.

Shrimp and Avocado Bruschetta

Makes 16 pieces:

16 large shrimp, peeled, deveined, and cooked
1 avocado
1 tomato
1 sprig cilantro
1 teaspoon freshly squeezed lemon juice
16 toasted baguette slices
Salt (preferably kosher or sea)
Freshly ground black pepper

Rinse shrimp, pat dry, and season with salt and pepper.

Remove the pit and skin from the avocado and gently mash the flesh. Rinse tomato, remove the seeds, and dice. Rinse cilantro, dry, remove the leaves, and chop finely. Combine the avocado, tomato, lemon juice, and cilantro.

Spread avocado on top of toasted baguette slices, top each with 1 shrimp, and sprinkle with cilantro.

Grilled Shrimp with Cocktail Sauce

Serves 2:

Cocktail sauce:
½ cup ketchup
1 tablespoon horseradish
1 teaspoon lemon juice
Freshly ground black pepper
Grilled shrimp:
24 uncooked, large shrimp, deveined and peeled, with tail intact
4 wooden skewers soaked in water
Juice of 1 lemon
Freshly ground black pepper

COCKTAIL SAUCE: In a bowl, combine ketchup, horseradish, and lemon. Stir together and season to taste with pepper. Cover and chill in the refrigerator until ready to serve.

GRILLED SHRIMP: Prepare gas grill to medium heat or preheat oven broiler.

Place 6 shrimp on each skewer. Brush with lemon juice and sprinkle with pepper. Cook for 6–7 minutes on each side. Serve on a bed of steamed white rice with lemon slices and cocktail sauce for dipping on the side.

Shrimp Salad

Serves 2:

1 pound shrimp, cooked, peeled, and deveined, chilled
1 pound grape tomatoes
1 avocado
1 cup cooked corn
2 tablespoons extra virgin olive oil
1 tablespoon red wine vinegar
Salt (preferably kosher or sea)
Freshly ground black pepper
2 cups mixed greens

Rinse shrimp and pat dry. Slice tomatoes in half and cube avocado into ½ inch pieces. In a bowl, combine shrimp, tomatoes, avocado, and corn. Drizzle with olive oil and vinegar, and season with salt and pepper. Toss well and serve on top of mixed greens.

Asian Noodles with Shrimp and Basil

Serves 2:

1 package Asian noodles (cellophane noodles)
1 pound shrimp, cooked, peeled, and deveined
½ bunch fresh basil
6–8 mint leaves
1 tablespoon lemon zest
½ small red bell pepper

Cook noodles according to package instructions, drain, and set aside.

Rinse shrimp and pat dry. Rinse basil and mint leaves, dry, and chop finely. Rinse lemon and zest. Rinse bell pepper, remove the seeds, and chop finely.

Thoroughly combine all ingredients in a bowl. Serve garnished with a lime wedge.

Spaghetti with Shrimp and Asparagus

Serves 4:

1 pound fresh asparagus, tips only
1 pound dry spaghetti
4 cloves garlic
½ cup extra virgin olive oil
1 cup butter
1 tablespoon lemon juice
1 pound medium shrimp, peeled and deveined
½ bunch fresh Italian parsley
Salt (preferably kosher or sea)
Freshly ground black pepper

In a small saucepan, boil asparagus in enough water to cover until bright green, about 4–5 minutes, drain, and set aside.

Bring a large pot with 4–5 quarts of salted water to full boil, place the spaghetti in the pot, and return to a rolling boil. Cook according to package directions until al dente. Drain well and set aside.

Peel garlic and mince. In a large saucepan, heat olive oil and sauté garlic until golden brown. Add butter and lemon juice, heat until melted, then add the shrimp to the saucepan, and cook until they turn pink. Add asparagus, stirring, and remove from heat.

Rinse parsley, dry, remove the leaves, and chop finely. In a large bowl, toss shrimp and asparagus with the spaghetti and season with salt and pepper. Add parsley and toss. Serve immediately.

Lobster Salad
with Basil Dressing

Serves 2:

1 cooked lobster (2 pounds)
4–5 sprigs fresh basil
2 tablespoons extra virgin olive oil
1 tablespoon lemon juice
2 cups mixed greens
Salt (preferably kosher or sea)
Freshly ground black pepper

Crack open lobster shell and carefully remove all of the meat, trying to keep it in tact.

Rinse basil, dry, remove leaves, and chop finely. In a large bowl, combine basil, olive oil and lemon juice, and season with salt and pepper. Add lobster meat to the bowl and toss until thoroughly coated.

Rinse greens, dry, then divide onto 2 plates, and arrange lobster pieces over the top. Garnish with additional chopped basil.

Lobster with Drawn Butter

Serves 4:

4 live lobsters (1½ pounds each)
2 lemons
2 limes
⅓ cup unsalted butter
Sea salt

Fill large stock pot with 1½–2½ gallons of water. Add salt and bring water to rapid boil. Drop in lobsters one at a time, head first, and return water to boil. Boil for 12–14 minutes or until lobsters are a bright red and the long antennae can be pulled loose with ease.

Remove lobsters with tongs and discard the liquid. Allow lobsters to drain.

Rinse lemons and limes and slice into 8 wedges. Melt butter in a saucepan, adding a pinch of salt if desired. Serve lobster with butter and lemon and lime wedges on the side.

Lobsters and Stuffed Tomatoes

Serves 4:

Stuffed tomatoes:
8 tomatoes (small to medium size)
1 bunch fresh Italian parsley
1 tablespoon extra virgin olive oil
1 clove garlic
2 tablespoons shelled almonds
2 tablespoons vegetable stock
2 tablespoons freshly grated Parmigiano-Reggiano
⅓ pound shrimp, cooked, peeled, and deveined
Sea salt
Freshly ground black pepper
Lobsters:
2 lobsters (1½–2 pounds each)
3 teaspoons sea salt

Preheat oven to 425°.

STUFFED TOMATOES: Wash tomatoes, cut off their tops, and remove the seeds with a small spoon. Arrange them in a greased baking dish, cut side up, and season with salt and pepper.

Rinse parsley, dry, and remove the leaves. In a blender, purée parsley leaves with olive oil, garlic, almonds, and stock. Stir in the Parmigiano-Reggiano and season with salt and pepper. Rinse shrimp, pat dry, and chop finely, then mix into the stuffing. Fill tomatoes with the stuffing and bake in the oven for about 15 minutes.

LOBSTERS: Fill large stock pot with 1½–2½ gallons of water. Add salt and bring water to rapid boil. Drop in lobsters one at a time, head first, and return water to boil. Boil for 12–14 minutes or until lobsters are a bright red and the long antennae can be pulled loose with ease.

Remove the lobsters, cool slightly, and cut each lobster in half lengthwise with a large knife. (Insert the tip of the knife into the breastplate from above and press down through the body. Break the claws by tapping with the back of the knife. Season with salt and pepper.)

Arrange one lobster half and one claw on each plate and serve with stuffed tomatoes.

Stuffed Lobster Tails

Serves 8:

8 cooked lobster tails (½–1 pounds each)
4–5 sprigs fresh Italian parsley
2 cups dry breadcrumbs
½ pound butter
2 teaspoons Worcestershire sauce
⅛ teaspoon salt (preferable kosher or sea)

Preheat oven to 325°F.

Remove the lobster meat from the tails and chop coarsely. Rinse parsley, dry, remove leaves, and chop finely. In a bowl, combine the lobster with parsley, breadcrumbs, butter, Worcestershire sauce, and salt.

Fill lobster tails with the stuffing. Place in a foil lined baking pan, bringing the edges of the foil over the tails.

Bake for 50 minutes. Remove from the oven and serve hot. Steamed green beans and fettuccini make for delicious side dishes.

Lobster
with Parmesan Risotto

Serves 4:

Lobster:
2 lobsters (about 1 pound each)
Sea salt
1 bay leaf
1 teaspoon peppercorns
Parmesan wafers:
⅔ cup freshly grated Parmigiano-Reggiano
Risotto:
2½ cups fish stock
1 onion
2 tablespoons butter
2 tablespoons olive oil
1½ cups Arborio rice
½ cup freshly grated Parmigiano-Reggiano
1 teaspoon grated lemon rind
Salt (preferably kosher or sea)
Freshly ground black pepper
Garnish:
1 tablespoon finely diced dried apricots
1 cup cooked soy beans
Dill tips

Preheat the oven to 350°F.

LOBSTER: Fill large stock pot with 1½–2½ gallons of water. Add salt, bay leaf, and peppercorns and bring water to rapid boil. Drop in lobsters one at a time, head first, and return water to boil. Boil for 12–14 minutes or until lobsters are a bright red and the long antennae can be easily pulled loose.

Remove the lobsters, cool slightly, and cut each lobster in half lengthwise with a large knife. (Insert the tip of the knife into the breastplate from above and press down through the body. Break the claws by tapping with the back of the knife. Season with salt and pepper.)

PARMESAN WAFERS: Place a 4 inch cookiecutter on a baking sheet lined with parchment paper, and spread a thin, even layer of grated cheese inside. Remove the cutter and form 3 more cheese circles the same way. Bake in the oven for about 5 minutes, until the cheese melts, bubbles, and turns golden brown. Remove from the oven to cool slightly, then remove from the parchment and place on a cake rack to crisp.

RISOTTO: Bring stock to a boil in a pot then lower the heat and keep warm. Peel onion and chop finely. In a large pot, heat butter and olive oil and sauté onion until translucent. Add rice and sauté, stirring. Gradually add the hot stock, ½ cup at a time, stirring constantly until the rice is cooked, about 18 minutes. Stir in the Parmigiano-Reggiano and lemon rind and season with salt and pepper.

Serve immediately. Spoon the risotto into bowls, arrange the lobster on top with Parmesan wafers on the side. Garnish with dried apricots, soy beans, and dill.

Mussels and Clams

Mussels and clams are filter feeding bivalves that are found both in fresh and salt water. Popular around the globe, these mollusks are versatile and although can be time consuming, quite simple to prepare. It is thought that mussels were the first seafood to be domesticated. There is evidence dating them back to the Roman Age and in the 13th century, the French were cultivating them for culinary usage. Clams, on the other hand, were first farmed in the 1930s and it wasn't until the 1960s that they gained a culinary foothold in the north eastern United States. And while these bivalves have different histories, one thing they have in common is a fabulous flavor when cooked to perfection.

When selecting mussels or clams, be sure they are as fresh as can be for the best quality and flavor. This means that they are alive at the time of purchase and their shells should be tightly closed, or they should close quickly when tapped. Avoid any that are smelly or have cracked shells. Once home, mussels and clams need to be cleaned. Since they were most recently living in the sea, they may have some residual sand inside them that needs to be washed away. Rinse under cold water and use a stiff brush to scrub the shells. Mussels will need to be debearded. Preparing mussels and clams is a relatively simple task; they can either be steamed or boiled. Once cooked, discard shells that are not open.

Steamed Mussels in White Wine

Serves 4:

48 fresh mussels
2 medium shallots
2 sprigs thyme
8 sprigs fresh Italian parsley
1 tomato
3 green onions
1½ cups dry white wine
½ cup butter
Salt (preferably kosher or sea)
Freshly ground black pepper

Scrub mussels under cold, running water, and debeard. Soak in cold water for about 20 minutes, drain, and discard any that are open.

Peel shallot and chop finely. Rinse thyme and parsley, dry, remove leaves, and chop finely. Rinse tomato, remove seeds, and dice. Rinse onions and slice into thin rings.

Combine wine, shallots, and thyme in a large pot and bring to simmer over medium heat for 4 minutes, then add mussels. Cover and turn heat to high. Steam for 8 minutes, or until mussels have opened, gently shaking the pot every minute, keeping the pot covered the entire time.

Using a slotted spoon, remove mussels from the pot being careful to discard any that have not opened. Set mussels aside in a deep bowl and cover with foil to keep warm. Add parsley and butter to the broth and stir until butter is melted, then add tomatoes, and green onions.

Ladle broth over mussels and garnish with a lemon wedge on the side. Sprinkle additional chopped parsley over the top.

Steamed Mussels
with Parsley and Onions

Serves 4:

48 fresh mussels
5 cloves garlic
2 onions
1 bunch fresh parsley
2 tablespoons extra virgin olive oil
1 cup white wine
2 tablespoons butter
Salt (preferably kosher or sea)
Freshly ground black pepper

Scrub mussels under cold, running water and debeard. Soak in cold water for about 20 minutes, drain, and discard any that are open.

Peel garlic and onion. Mince garlic and slice onion. Rinse parsley, dry, remove leaves, and chop finely. Heat olive oil in a large stockpot over medium-low heat. Add garlic and sauté for 1 minute, but do not brown. Add onion and cook until almost tender, then add the wine. Stir in parsley and butter and season with salt and pepper. Add mussels, cover, and cook until the shells are opened, about 10 minutes. Discard any unopened shells.

Divide mussels and broth between 4 deep bowls and garnish with additional parsley.

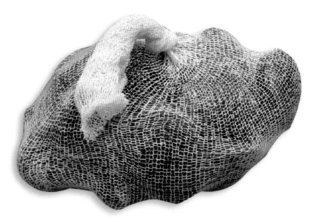

Mussels Napoli

Serves 4:

48 fresh mussels
1 onion
2 cloves garlic
½ small leek
1 small carrot
1 tablespoon finely chopped parsley
1 tablespoon finely chopped basil leaves
1 can diced tomatoes (15 ounces)
½ cup extra virgin olive oil
Salt (preferably kosher or sea)
Freshly ground black pepper

Wash and scrub the mussels thoroughly under cold running water and debeard if necessary. Discard any that are already open.

Peel onion and garlic. Finely dice the onion and finely chop the garlic. Wash and trim leek cutting white and pale green parts into rings. Peel and finely dice carrot. Rinse parsley and basil, dry, remove leaves, and chop finely.

Heat oil in a large stockpot. Sauté onion and garlic until translucent, stirring, then add the carrot, and sauté for 2 minutes. Add the leek and tomatoes and cook gently for 2–3 more minutes. Finally add mussels, parsley and basil, cover, and cook for about 8 minutes, until the mussels have opened, shaking the pan vigorously from time to time. Discard any mussels that have not opened.

Serve mussels in a large dish sprinkled with additional parsley leaves and chopped basil.

Mussels in Dill Broth

Serves 4:

48 fresh mussels
3 cloves garlic
1 large yellow onion
1 tablespoon extra virgin olive oil
2½ cups dry white wine
3 bay leaves
2 sprigs fresh dill
½ cup milk
2 egg yolks
½ cup heavy cream
Freshly ground black pepper

Wash and scrub the mussels thoroughly under cold running water and debeard if necessary. Discard any that are already open.

Peel garlic and onion and chop finely. In a large pot, heat olive oil and sauté garlic and onion until translucent but not browned. Add wine and bay leaves, stir, and season with pepper. Add mussels and steam until the shells have opened, about 8–10 minutes. Remove mussels to a large serving bowl, discarding any unopened shells, and set the broth aside.

Rinse dill, dry, and chop. In a saucepan, heat milk, add 1 cup of the reserved broth, and stir in dill.

Beat egg yolks and temper with a spoonful or two of broth. Over very low heat, stir beaten egg yolks into the milk. When the sauce thickens, add cream. If the sauce is too thick, add more broth until it becomes the consistency that you desire.

Divide mussels into 4 deep bowls, pour dill broth over the top, and garnish with a sprig of dill. Serve with crusty baguette slices, a lemon wedge, and a glass of white wine.

Mussels with Mustard Sauce

Serves 4:

4 large Idaho potatoes
⅔ cup butter
2 tablespoons mustard
⅔ cup heavy cream
⅛ teaspoon cayenne pepper
48 fresh mussels
3 onions
1 leek
1 bunch parsley
1 tablespoon extra virgin olive oil
1 cup dry white wine
Salt (preferably kosher or sea)
Freshly ground white pepper
½ bunch arugula

Peel and wash potatoes, then cut out balls using a melon baller. Boil potato balls in salted water for about 20 minutes and drain thoroughly.

In a large saucepan, melt butter with mustard, stirring. Whisk in cream and season with cayenne pepper. Add potatoes to the sauce and keep warm.

Wash and scrub the mussels thoroughly under cold running water and debeard, if necessary. Discard any that are already open.

Peel and chop onions. Trim, wash, and dice leek, white part only. Wash parsley, dry, remove leaves, and chop finely.

In a large stockpot, heat olive oil and sauté onions until translucent, then add leek. Stir in parsley, 1 cup of water, and wine. Season with salt and pepper and bring to a boil. Add mussels to the pot, cover, and cook over high heat for about 8 minutes, shaking the pan vigorously from time to time. Drain mussels, discarding any that have not opened.

Stir potatoes into the pot, divide into 4 deep bowls, and serve. Garnish with arugula.

Mussels in Curry Sauce

Serves 4:

48 fresh mussels
1 can whole tomatoes (15 ounces)
1 medium onion
2 tablespoons extra virgin olive oil
1 tablespoon finely chopped fresh ginger
1 tablespoon ground coriander
1 teaspoon turmeric
1 teaspoon red pepper flakes
½ cup white wine
Coarse sea salt
Juice of 1 lemon
4 sprigs fresh cilantro

Rinse the mussels and wash and scrub the mussels thoroughly under cold, running water and debeard, if necessary. Discard any that are already open.

Drain tomatoes, reserving ½ cup of the liquid. Peel onion and chop finely. Heat olive oil in a deep pot and add onion, stirring over high heat until they turn light brown, about 5 minutes. Lower heat and stir in ginger, coriander, turmeric, and red pepper flakes. Cook for 1 more minute, then add tomatoes, reserved tomato liquid, wine, and mussels, season with salt, and bring to a boil. Cover the pot and steam until mussels open, about 7–8 minutes. Discard any mussels that do not open.

Transfer mussels and broth to 4 deep bowls. Sprinkle with lemon juice and cilantro. Serve immediately with Naan or other flat bread.

Linguine with Mussels

Serves 4:

48 fresh mussels
1 pound linguine
1 small onion
2 cloves garlic
6–8 sprigs fresh parsley
2 tablespoons extra virgin olive oil
1 bay leaf
¼ teaspoon dried thyme
2 cups white wine
2 tablespoons butter

Wash and scrub mussels thoroughly under cold running water and debeard, if necessary. Discard any that are already open.

Bring a large pot of lightly salted water to a boil. Add linguine and cook for 8–10 minutes or until al dente, drain, and set aside.

Peel onion and garlic and chop. Rinse, dry, remove leaves, and finely chop parsley. In a large pot, heat olive oil and sauté onion, garlic, parsley, bay leaf, thyme, and wine. Bring to a boil and lower heat; cook for 2 minutes. Add mussels; cover and cook just until they open, 7–8 minutes. Be careful not to overcook and discard mussels that do not open.

Divide linguini into 4 bowls and arrange mussels on top.

Strain broth through a fine-meshed sieve and return to the pot. Add butter and heat until it melts. Pour over mussels immediately and serve.

New England Clam Chowder

Serves 4:

4 slices bacon
1 small onion
4 potatoes
1 tablespoon all-purpose flour
1 cup bottled clam juice
1 cup half-and-half
2 cans minced clams (6½ ounces each)
Salt (preferably kosher or sea)
Freshly ground black pepper
½ cup heavy cream (optional)

In a large saucepan over medium-high heat, fry the bacon until crisp, about 10 minutes. Drain on paper towels, reserving the fat in the pan, crumble, and set aside.

Peel and chop onion and peel and cube potato. Using the same saucepan, sauté onion and potatoes for 3–5 minutes. Sprinkle with flour and stir to coat. Add clam juice, bring to a boil, reduce heat to low, and simmer for about 15 minutes or until potatoes are tender, then add half-and-half, clams and bacon, and season to taste with salt and pepper. Finally, whisk in heavy cream, if desired and allow to heat through, but not to boil, about 5 minutes.

To serve, ladle chowder into warm bowls and grind a little pepper on the top.

Manhattan Clam Chowder

Serves 4:

36 little neck clams
5 slices bacon
1 medium onion
2 stalks celery
½ bell pepper
3 cups water
2 russet potatoes
3 carrots
3 sprigs fresh parsley
1 teaspoon sea salt
½ teaspoon dried thyme leaves
⅛ teaspoon freshly ground black pepper
1 can diced tomatoes (15 ounces), undrained
1 bay leaf

Wash and scrub clams thoroughly under cold, running water. Discard any that are open. In a large stockpot bring 2 cups of water to a boil. Add clams, cover, and cook for 5 minutes. Uncover and quickly stir the clams with a wooden spoon, then replace the lid. Allow clams to cook 5–10 minutes longer or until most have opened. Transfer clams to a large bowl or baking dish and strain broth through a fine-meshed sieve into a bowl. When clams are cool enough to handle, remove them from their shells. Discard clams with unopened shells. Set clams and broth aside.

Fry bacon in large pot over medium heat until crisp. Remove, drain on paper towels, and then crumble into pieces. Set aside. Leave about 2 tablespoons of bacon renderings in the pot.

Peel and chop onion. Rinse and chop celery, remove the seeds from bell pepper, and chop, peel, and dice potatoes and carrots. Rinse parsley, dry, remove leaves, and chop finely.

In the same pot, reheat bacon fat, add onions, celery and bell pepper, and cook until tender, stirring. Add water, potatoes, carrots, parsley, salt, thyme, pepper, reserved clam broth, tomatoes, and bay leaf. Bring to a boil. Reduce heat to low; cover and simmer 25–35 minutes or until vegetables are tender.

Remove bay leaf. Stir in clams and bacon. Cook until thoroughly heated, stirring frequently, careful not to boil, about 5 minutes.

Serve Manhattan Clam Chowder in bowls garnished with a sprig of thyme and traditional oyster crackers on the side.

New England Clam Bake

Serves 4:

4 ears corn on the cob
1 tablespoon kosher salt
24 fresh clams
2 tablespoons cornmeal
2 live lobsters (1 pound each)
4 red new potatoes

Remove husks from corn and discard the silks. Cut corn in half. Place husks and corn in a large bowl. Cover with cold water and sprinkle with salt. Soak for 1 hour.

Scrub clams with a stiff brush under cold running water to remove all sand. Discard any that are open. Half fill a large bowl with water, stir in cornmeal, and add the clams. Add more water if needed to cover the calms. Let stand for 30 minutes to disgorge any sand inside. Drain and rinse well.

Fill large stock pot with 1½–2½ gallons of water. Add salt and bring water to rapid boil. Drop in lobsters one at a time, head first, and return water to boil. Boil for 12–14 minutes or until lobsters are a bright red and the long antennae can be pulled loose with ease. Reserve 6 cups of the cooking liquid.

Place a steamer rack or basket in the bottom of the same pot. Drain the corn and husks. Cover the rack or basket with half of the cornhusks. Cut potatoes in half. Place corn and potatoes on top of the husks. Add reserved liquid and top with remaining husks. Bring to a boil over high heat. Reduce the heat to low and simmer, covered, for 20 minutes.

While potatoes and corn are cooking, cut the lobster in half lengthwise. Hold lobster halves under running water to clean and remove the entrails.

During the last 5 minutes of cooking corn and potatoes, place lobster halves and clams in the pot on top of the husks. Cover, and simmer for 5–8 minutes, or until the clams open. Discard any unopened clams before serving.

Place half of a lobster in each of 4 shallow bowls. Arrange 6 clams, 2 pieces of corn, and 2 potatoes around the lobster. Serve lemon wedges on the side.

Clams in Tomato Sauce

Serves 4:

3 pounds clams
6 sprigs fresh Italian parsley
4 cloves garlic
4 tablespoon butter
1½ pounds diced tomatoes
1 bottle dry white wine
1 green onion
Salt (preferably kosher or sea)
Freshly ground black pepper

Wash and scrub the clams thoroughly under cold, running water. Discard any that are open.

Peel and mince garlic. Rinse parsley, dry, remove leaves, and chop finely. Heat butter in a saucepan and sauté garlic 2–3 minutes. Stir in tomatoes, season with salt and pepper, simmer for about 3 minutes, then add 1 cup of wine, and simmer for 3 more minutes. Add parsley and season with salt and pepper.

Place clams into a large pot with remaining wine. Cover and cook for about 8 minutes. Remove clams from the pot, discarding any that are still closed, and mix with tomato sauce and a little cooking liquid.

Wash and trim onion and cut into thin strips. Serve clams in deep bowls with tomato sauce, onion strips, and a lemon wedge.

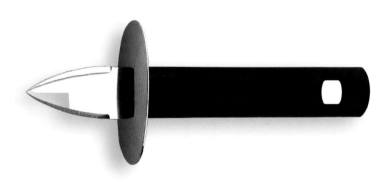

Clams in Pesto Broth

Serves 2:

24 fresh clams
½ cup rice
½ bunch fresh Italian parsley
½ bunch fresh basil leaves
3 cloves garlic
⅓ cup extra virgin olive oil
1 cup water
½ cup fish stock
Salt (preferably kosher or sea)
Freshly ground black pepper

Wash and scrub the clams thoroughly in a pot under cold, running water. Discard any that are open.

Put rice into a pan with 1 cup of lightly salted water and bring to a boil. Cover and simmer gently over low heat for about 25 minutes.

Rinse parsley and basil, dry, remove leaves, and chop finely. Peel garlic and chop finely.

In a deep pot, heat ½ cup olive oil and sauté garlic without browning. Add clams and sauté for 3 minutes until all the shells have opened. Discard any that have not. Add water and fish stock and cook over low heat for 4 minutes.

Transfer clams to a bowl and strain the broth through a fine sieve to remove any traces of sand. Return clams to the broth; add parsley, basil, remaining olive oil, and season with salt and pepper.

Serve clams on top of rice in deep bowls. Garnish with additional chopped parsley and basil.

Clams in Garlic and White Wine Broth

Serves 2:

50 small clams
6 cloves garlic
2 tablespoons extra virgin olive oil
1 cup white wine
2 tablespoons butter
½ bunch fresh Italian parsley

Rinse and scrub clams under cold running water, discarding any that remain open.

Peel and mince garlic. In a large pot, heat olive oil over medium heat. Add garlic; sauté for 1 minute, or until tender, then add the wine. Boil until wine has reduced by half. Add clams, cover, and steam until they start to open. Add butter, cover, and cook until most clams open. Discard those that do not open.

Transfer clams and broth to 2 large bowls. Sprinkle with parsley and serve a toasted baguette to soak up the broth.

Linguine in Clam Sauce

Serves 4:

2 dozen littleneck clams
1 cup white wine
1 pound dry linguine
1 small red onion
3 cloves garlic
½ bunch fresh Italian parsley
⅓ cup extra virgin olive oil
½ cup chopped tomatoes
2 tablespoons fresh lemon juice
Salt (preferably kosher or sea)

Wash and scrub clams thoroughly under cold, running water removing any sand. Soak for 20 minutes, discarding any that do not open.

Bring large pot of salted water to a boil over high heat. Add linguine and cook according to package instructions until al dente.

Place a skillet with a tight fitting lid over high heat. When pan is hot, add clams and ½ cup of wine. Place lid on pot and steam until they open, about 5–8 minutes. Remove clams and reduce liquid slightly. Strain liquid and reserve.

Peel onion and garlic and chop finely. Rinse parsley, dry, remove leaves, and chop finely. Heat olive oil in a large pot. Add onion and cook on medium-low heat for about 5 minutes or until softened. Add garlic and cook for 1 minute, then add reserved clam liquid, and remaining wine. Reduce for a couple of minutes, then add the cooked clams and tomatoes and cook just until heated through. Remove pot from the heat and stir in lemon juice and parsley.

Add linguine to the pot and toss with the clams and sauce until thoroughly coated.

Serve immediately in warm bowls with crusty bread to soak up the extra sauce.

Scallops and Oysters

Scallops and oysters, like mussels and clams are also part of the bivalve mollusk family. There are hundreds of types of scallops and they are usually sold shucked and out of their shell. If you have the opportunity to purchase scallops in the shell, do so and you will be able to see and sample the bright orange roe that is attached to them, which is a treat. Scallops range from small, sweet, delicate bay scallops that are great tossed in noodles (p. 104) or even enjoyed raw, to large sea scallops that are well suited for searing and wrapping bacon around (p. 100).

Oysters, largely known for their aphrodisiac powers (which Roman emperors reportedly paid for by their weight in gold), are the one mollusk that is most likely to be consumed raw. In fact, standing ankle deep in a bed of oysters with a shucking knife is something any oyster fan should experience at least once in their life. But until that fantasy can be realized, serve fresh oysters au natural, on a bed of ice with a squeeze of lemon juice, and a dip in Mignonette Sauce (p. 108). Oysters also make a rich and meaty addition to a stew (p. 116) or gratin.

Bacon Wrapped Scallops

Serves 4:

16 large sea scallops
8 slices bacon, cut in half
2 tablespoon extra virgin olive oil
Juice of 1 lemon
1 teaspoon fresh cracked black pepper
12 grape tomatoes
1 cup arugula
16 toothpicks

Preheat oven broiler.

Wrap a slice of bacon around each scallop securing with a toothpick. Place scallops on a baking sheet and broil in the oven until golden brown and bacon is done to desired crispness, about 5–6 minutes.

Meanwhile, combine olive oil, lemon juice, and cracked pepper in a small bowl. Slice tomatoes in half and toss with arugula and dressing until coated.

Divide arugula and tomatoes onto 4 plates and serve bacon wrapped scallops on top.

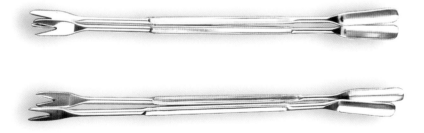

Seared Scallops
with Pea Sauce

Serves 4:

Pea sauce:
2 medium shallots
1 clove garlic
2 tablespoons extra virgin olive oil
½ cup butter
1 cup peas
½ cup white wine
½ cup fish stock
Ravioli and scallops:
1 package of fresh, large ravioli (16 ounces)
½ cup extra virgin olive oil
12 large sea scallops
Salt (preferably kosher or sea)
Freshly ground black pepper

FOR THE PEA SAUCE: Peel shallots and garlic and mince. In a large skillet, heat 1 tablespoon of olive oil with the butter over medium heat. Add shallots and garlic and sauté until translucent. Add peas, wine, and stock and bring to a boil over high heat. Reduce heat to medium and continue cooking for 10–15 minutes or until the peas are tender and bright green. Remove from the heat, transfer to a blender, and purée until smooth. Season with salt and pepper to taste, then add remaining olive oil. Set aside.

FOR THE RAVIOLI AND SCALLOPS: In a large pot, bring 4–5 quarts of lightly salted water to a boil and cook ravioli according to package instructions. Drain and toss lightly with 1 tablespoon olive oil. Set aside.

Rinse scallops, pat dry, score, and season with salt and pepper. Heat remaining olive oil in a large, nonstick skillet over medium-high heat until very hot, but not smoking. Add scallops, making sure not to overcrowd the pan, and sauté on the first side until nicely browned, 3–4 minutes. Turn to the other side and cook for 1 more minute.

Reheat the pea sauce, if necessary, in a small saucepan over low heat. Arrange 3 raviolis on each plate and top each with 1 scallop and drizzle the pea sauce in the center.

Thai Noodle Salad with Grilled Scallops

Serves 4:

4 ounces rice noodles
2 tablespoons soya oil
2 green onions
8 fresh cilantro sprigs
4 mint leaves
1 mango
⅓ pound Chinese cabbage (about 10 leaves)
2 tablespoons freshly squeezed lime juice
2 tablespoons freshly squeezed orange juice
12 sea scallops with shells
2 tablespoons freshly squeezed lemon juice
Salt (preferably kosher or sea)
Freshly ground black pepper
12 cherry tomatoes

Cook noodles in salted water until al dente. Drain, refresh in cold water, and set aside to cool.

Rinse onion, cilantro, and mint, dry then chop. Peel mango, cut flesh away from the stone, and dice. Shred cabbage. Mix oil, onions, cilantro, mint, lime juice, orange juice, mango, and cabbage and add to the noodles. Combine until noodles are thoroughly coated and season with salt and extra lime juice.

Wash scallops under cold, running water, insert a short knife between the shells, and run it around to separate. Remove the top shell and loosen the flesh with a knife. Remove the gray edges and the orange coral from the white flesh. Wash the scallops thoroughly several times.

Sprinkle scallops with lemon juice and season with salt and pepper. Cook scallops on the grill or in a nonstick grill pan (not too hot) for 1–2 minutes on each side. Grill the tomatoes for a few minutes.

To serve, put the noodles into the center of a serving dish and arrange the tomatoes and scallops around it. Garnish with additional chopped cilantro and basil leaves.

Oyster Canapés

Serves 4:

12 fresh oysters
1 crusty baguette
1 tomato
2 tablespoons extra virgin olive oil
Juice of ½ lemon
12 fine pieces of lemon zest
Freshly ground black pepper

Preheat oven broiler.

Scrub oysters under cold water with a stiff brush to remove the dirt, especially in the hinge area where mud has a tendency to get trapped and open with an oyster knife. (Hold oyster in one hand in a kitchen cloth, rounded side down, and insert the point of an oyster knife next to the hinge. Twist to open and slide the knife along inside the top shell to release the muscle attaching the oyster to the shell. Remove the top shell, then loosen the oyster from the bottom shell.) Remove the oysters from their shells and drain on paper towels.

Slice baguette into 12 (1 inch) slices. Place on a baking sheet and toast under the broiler until golden. Remove and wrap in foil to keep warm.

Rinse tomato, remove seeds, and dice. Heat olive oil in a skillet over medium heat and cook the oysters for 1–2 minutes, so that they stew rather than fry. Sprinkle with lemon juice and season with pepper. Remove oysters from the skillet, place one on each baguette slice, scatter with diced tomatoes, and garnish each with a piece of lemon zest.

Oysters on the Half Shell

Serves 4:

24 fresh oysters
4 cups finely crushed ice
¼ cup kosher salt
Mignonette sauce:
1 large shallot
2 teaspoons finely crushed white pepper
⅛ teaspoon salt
¼ cup dry red wine
2 tablespoons olive oil

Scrub oysters under cold water with a stiff brush to remove the dirt, especially in the hinge area where mud has a tendency to get trapped and open with oyster knife. (Hold the oyster in one hand in a kitchen cloth, rounded side down, and insert the point of an oyster knife next to the hinge. Twist to open and slide the knife along inside the top shell to release the muscle attaching the oyster to the shell. Remove the top shell, then loosen the oyster from the bottom shell.)

Arrange the ice on a shallow, rimmed platter and press down gently to make a level bed. Sprinkle salt over the ice. Place oysters in their shells on the bed.

FOR THE MIGNONETTE SAUCE: Peel shallot and chop finely. In a small bowl, combine shallot, pepper, salt, wine and olive oil, and whisk to blend.

Place the sauce in a small, decorative bowl and serve with the oysters. If desired, serve cocktail sauce with horseradish alongside, too.

Oysters Rockefeler

Serves 4:

24 fresh oysters
6 cups rock salt
1 large shallot
½ bunch fresh parsley
1 bunch fresh tarragon
1 cup unsalted butter, at room temperature
⅓ cup water
2 cups spinach leaves, packed
Salt (preferably kosher or sea)
Freshly ground black pepper
Cayenne pepper
1 tablespoon Pernod

Preheat the oven to 450°F.

Scrub oysters under cold water with a stiff brush to remove the dirt, especially in the hinge area where mud has a tendency to get trapped and open with an oyster knife. (Hold the oyster in one hand in a kitchen cloth, rounded side down, and insert the point of an oyster knife next to the hinge. Twist to open and slide the knife along inside the top shell to release the muscle attaching the oyster to the shell. Remove the top shell, then loosen the oyster from the bottom shell.)

Place oysters in their shells on a bed of rock salt (about 1½ inches deep) in one or more baking pans. Set aside. (The rock salt keeps the oysters upright and holds the heat while they are cooking.)

Peel and mince shallots. Rinse, pat dry, and finely chop parsley and tarragon. Combine 4 tablespoons of butter with water and shallots in a saucepan and simmer until they are limp and the water has boiled away, about 5 minutes, making sure not to brown the shallots. Add spinach, parsley, and tarragon. Heat until spinach has wilted, just a few seconds. It must not actually cook and season with salt, pepper, and cayenne.

Purée spinach, Pernod, and remaining butter in a food processor or blender until smooth, then scoop a dollop on top of each oyster.

Bake oysters on the middle oven rack until the sauce is bubbly, about 5 minutes, being careful not to overcook.

Serve on a platter with lemon wedges.

Oysters with Tomato Oil

Serves 2:

2 tomatoes
2 cups extra virgin olive oil
12 fresh oysters
1 jalapeño pepper

Rinse tomatoes, remove seeds, and dice. Place tomatoes and oil in a pot and bring to a boil. Remove from heat and cool. Once cooled, pour into a blender or food processor, blend until smooth, then strain through a sieve, or cheesecloth. Set aside.

Scrub oysters under cold water with a stiff brush to remove the dirt, especially in the hinge area where mud has a tendency to get trapped and open with an oyster knife. (Hold the oyster in one hand in a kitchen cloth, rounded side down, and insert the point of an oyster knife next to the hinge. Twist to open and slide the knife along inside the top shell to release the muscle attaching the oyster to the shell. Remove the top shell, then loosen the oyster from the bottom shell.)

Rinse jalapeño, slice into 12 rings, and remove the seeds. Arrange oysters on a platter, drizzle tomato oil over the top, and garnish each with one slice of jalapeño.

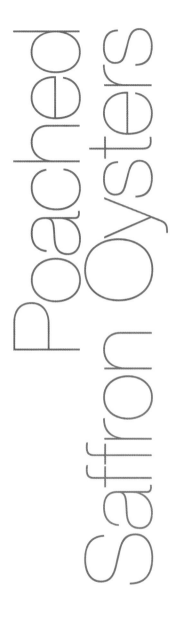

Poached Saffron Oysters

Serves 2:

24 oysters
3 medium leeks
2 tablespoons unsalted butter
1 cup water
3 cloves garlic
1 tablespoon extra virgin olive oil
1/8 teaspoon crumbled plus 1/2 teaspoon whole saffron threads
32 ounces bottled clam juice
1 cup whipping cream
3 tablespoons Pernod
Lemon zest, thinly sliced

Scrub oysters under cold water with a stiff brush to remove the dirt, especially in the hinge area where mud has a tendency to get trapped, and open with an oyster knife. (Hold the oyster in one hand in a kitchen cloth, rounded side down, and insert the point of an oyster knife next to the hinge. Twist to open and slide the knife along inside the top shell to release the muscle attaching the oyster to the shell. Remove the top shell, then loosen the oyster from the bottom shell.)

Rinse leeks and dice finely (white parts only). Melt butter in heavy skillet over medium heat. Add leeks and sauté until golden, about 10 minutes. Stir in water and purée in a blender until smooth. Set aside.

Peel and mince garlic. Heat oil in a heavy, large saucepan over medium heat. Add garlic and crumbled saffron and sauté for 1 minute. Add clam juice, cream and Pernod, and bring to a simmer, about 3–4 minutes. Add leek purée and return to a simmer for 1–2 more minutes.

Spoon the broth over each oyster, filling the shell. Sprinkle lemon and whole saffron threads on the top and serve immediately.

Oyster Stew

Serves 4:

16 ounces canned oysters, undrained
3 cups half-and-half
1 cup scaled milk
Pinch of cayenne pepper
½ cup unsalted butter, at room temperature
1 bay leaf
Sea salt
Hungarian sweet paprika

Pour liquid off the oysters and reserve.

In a bowl, combine half-and-half, milk, cayenne pepper, and season with salt.

In a medium-sized saucepan, melt 2 tablespoons of butter over medium heat and add the oysters. Cook gently, stirring occasionally, until they plump, about 5 minutes.

Pour the reserved oyster liquid, half-and-half, and bay leaf, into the saucepan. Heat, stirring, and simmer gently for 3 or 4 minutes until edges of the oysters curl. Be careful not to boil or overcook, oysters become tough!

Ladle the stew into heated soup bowls and swirl a dab of butter into each. Sprinkle with a dash of paprika. Serve at once with traditional oyster crackers.